backstreet boys

I'd like to thank the following:

KBNHA for welcoming me into their world and for their help and loyalty over the years.

Nina Bueti for her hard work in making this project come true. For her unfailing help on the road in keeping me sane, as well as for the long hours spent editing and supervising this book.

Denise McLean for her friendship, her trust, and for being there when it mattered.

Polsia Ryder for her vision and understanding.

BSB crews past and present and the illustrious members of the back lounge.

Also Nicole Peltz; Dave Wainwright for his invaluable help; Charley Prick; Bert Meyer; Rob Hallett; Ray Edwards; David Zedeck and family; The Firm; Beverly Horowitz, Diana Capriotti, Andrew Smith, Gabriel X. Ashkenazi, Janet Parker, Phyllis Mandel, Saho Fujii, and all at Random House; and Brad Foltz.

A special thanks to Gwen, Ione, and Harry for their patience and support.

And to all the nonbelievers over the years: BAH HUMBUG.

—Andre Csillag

Published by Delacorte Press
an imprint of Random House Children's Books
a division of Random House, Inc.
1540 Broadway, New York, New York 10036

Visit us on the Web! www.randomhouse.com/teens
Educators and librarians, for a variety of teaching tools, visit us at www.randomhouse.com/teachers

Library of Congress Cataloging-in-Publication Data
ISBN: 0-385-32800-1
Cataloging-in-Publication Data is available from the U.S. Library of Congress.

Book design by Bradford Foltz
Manufactured in the United States of America
July 2000
10 9 8 7 6 5 4 3 2 1
BVG

When I met the Backstreet Boys, it was relatively early in their career, in late 1995, doing a magazine shoot. I then worked with them several more times throughout 1996.

By 1997 the Boys had become so successful and the demand for photos of them so great from media all over the world that they needed their own official photographer. So in early 1997 I joined the BSB European tour, and I'm still with the Boys today.

We've traveled the world together. From Europe to Asia, from South America to Canada and the United States, I have been documenting their career in photographs. Kevin, Howie, Nick, Brian, and AJ have been gracious enough to let me tag along even in their downtime. I've been able to capture special moments behind the scenes and out of the spotlight because the Boys let me into their inner circle.

Now we're happy to open that circle to you, the fans, with this one-and-only Official Book. Some pictures may seem familiar, but most will be brand new. In their private moments and their public appearances, here are the Backstreet Boys, along with personal stories in their own words.

We hope you truly enjoy this book, because we created it for you.

—Andre Csillag

WE'RE STANDING IN FRONT OF BIG BEN IN LONDON, DOING PROMOTION. THESE ARE OUR FIRST TOUR JACKETS. WE LOOK LIKE A BASKETBALL TEAM. AS YOU CAN SEE, I DON'T HAVE FACIAL HAIR AND MY HAIR IS ITS NORMAL COLOR. —AJ

HERE'S BRIAN ACTING LIKE A GOOFBALL WEARING A U.K. POLICEMAN'S HAT. —NICK

HOW MANY BACKSTREET BOYS CAN YOU FIT INTO A PHONE BOOTH? —BRIAN

I WAS EXTREMELY SMALL BACK THEN SO THEY COULD PICK ME UP.
THEY CAN'T DO THAT NOW! —NICK

RECREATION TIME. WE DIDN'T GET OUT A LOT BACK THEN BECAUSE WE WERE
TRAVELING AND WORKING REAL HARD. SO WHEN YOU GOT US TOGETHER OUTSIDE,
WE ALWAYS DID SOME CRAZY STUFF. —BRIAN

WE USED TO THINK WE WERE COOL WEARING THOSE WHITE SHIRTS. —BRIAN

YEAH, REMEMBER THOSE VESTS? —NICK

I REMEMBER THIS SHRINE IN JAPAN WHERE YOU WROTE YOUR
WISHES ON A SMALL PIECE OF PAPER AND PLACED THEM
IN A TREE. WE DID IT, AND I THINK A LOT OF US HOPED FOR
SUCCESS IN THE U.S., AND IT FINALLY CAME TRUE. —NICK

I HAVE A REALLY BAD HAIRCUT. SO DO NICK, KEV, AND HOWIE. WE ARE IN TOKYO ON PROMO. I ATTEMPTED TO DYE
MY OWN HAIR AND AS YOU CAN TELL, IT TURNED OUT LOOKING LIKE CARAMEL. NICK LOOKS LIKE HE SHOULD BE IN
HANSON AND HOWIE IN MENUDO. —AJ

WE WERE TRYING TO BE BEAVIS AND BUTT-HEAD. NICK MESSING WITH MY HAIR.
I DIDN'T REALLY CARE FOR THE FOOD, SO WE AMUSED OURSELVES WITH OTHER
THINGS. CHOPSTICKS—LOOK, HA, HA. IT SEEMED FUNNY BACK THEN. —BRIAN

OUR PRESS SHOT AT THE EUROPEAN MTV AWARDS IN 1996, WHERE WE WON THE "BEST NEWCOMER" AWARD. —HOWIE

WE WON OUR VERY FIRST MTV EUROPE AWARD. IF YOU EVER GET A CHANCE TO SEE THE FOOTAGE OF THIS, WATCH IT.
HOWIE'S SPEECH WAS ABSOLUTELY HILARIOUS. HE STUTTERED, CHOKED, COUGHED, AND FINALLY BLURTED OUT,
"WE WANT TO THANK GOD." —AJ

WE'RE ALL BABY FACES. —KEVIN

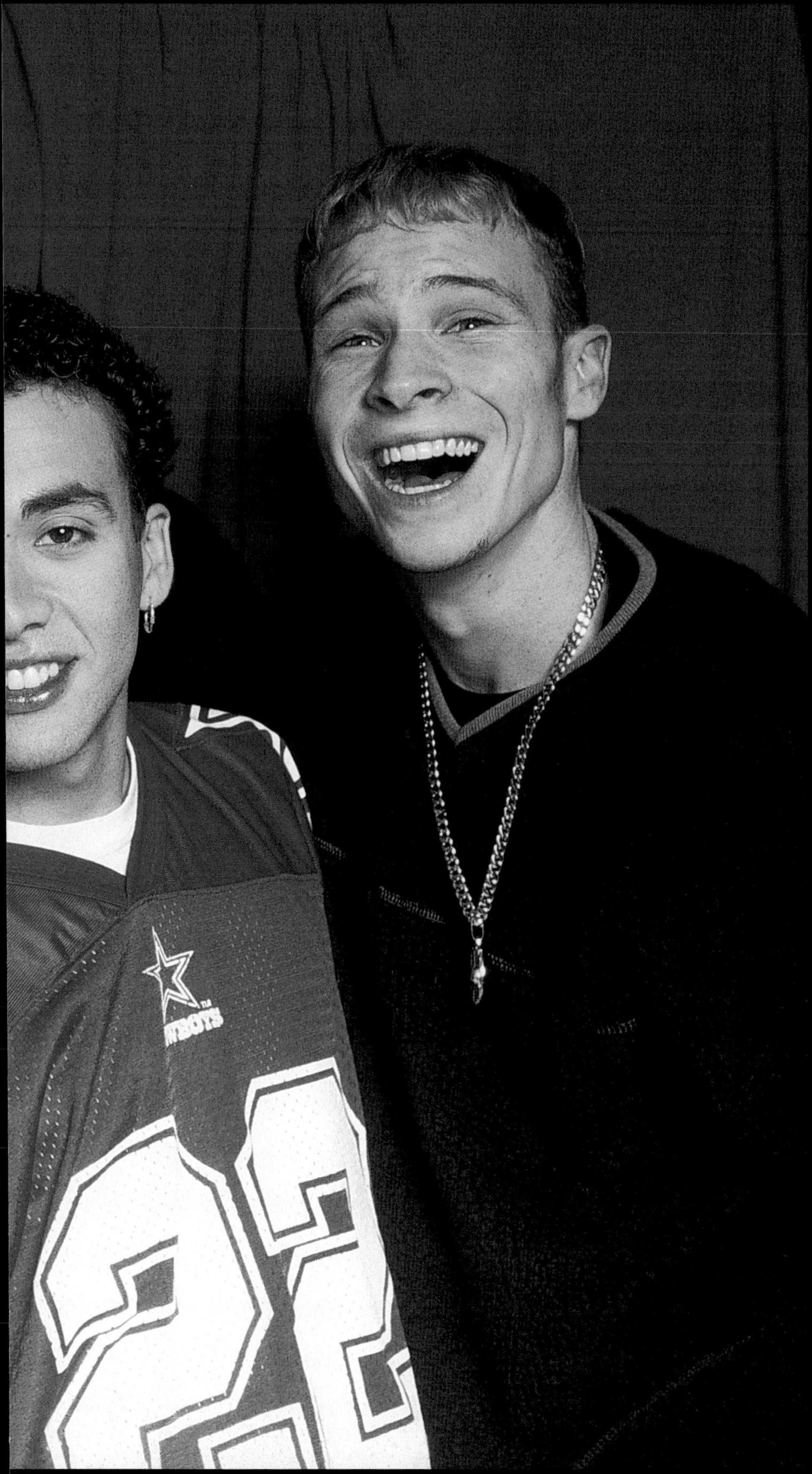

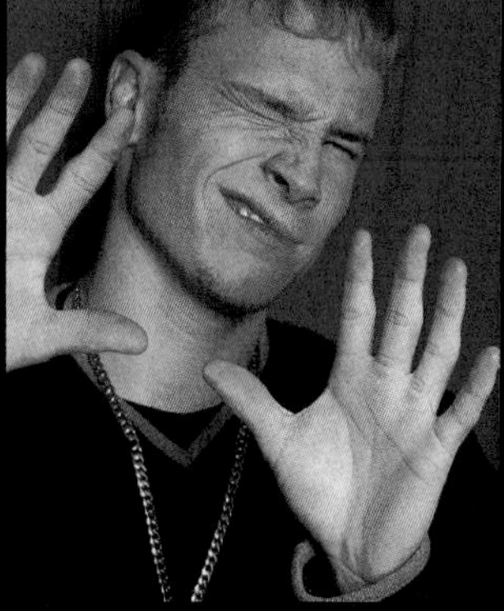

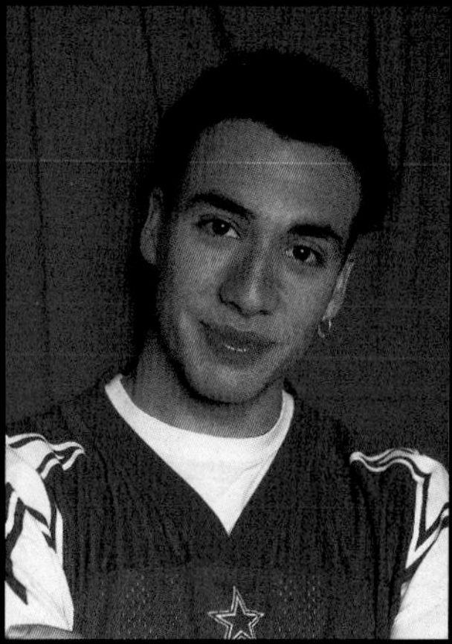

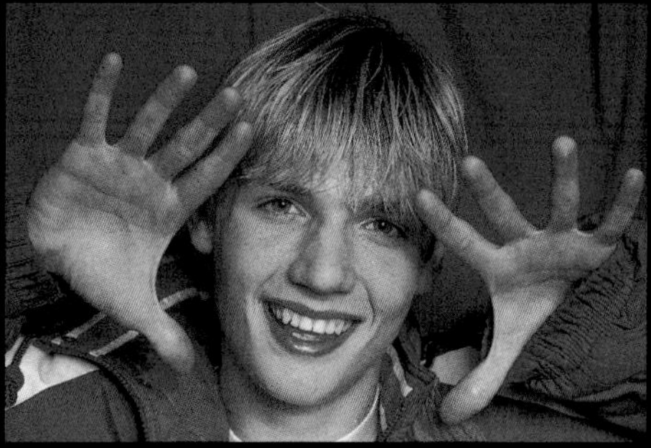

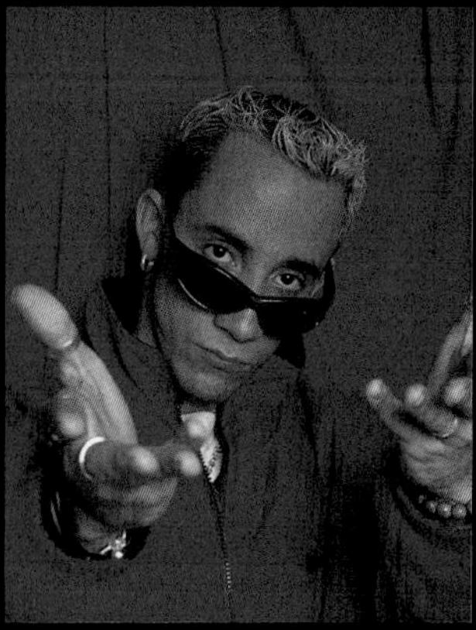

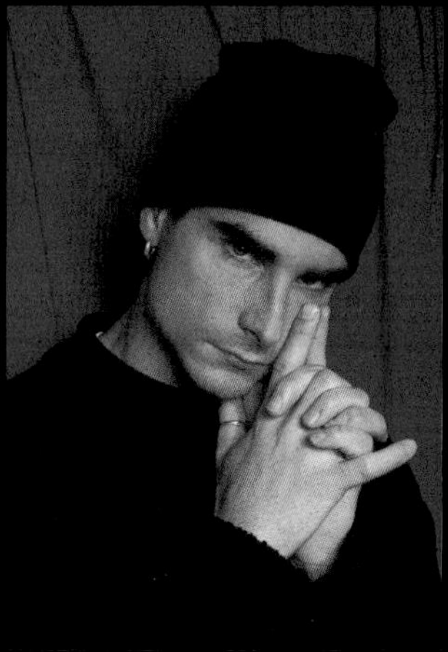

"NOBODY BUT YOU."
OUR SECOND EUROPEAN TOUR. —KEVIN

DOING A CAPPELLA NUMBERS BY
GROUPS THAT INSPIRED US. —AJ

THIS WAS OUR GERMAN TOUR IN
FEBRUARY 1997. —HOWIE

HAPPY BIRTHDAY TO ME, TWENTY-TWO!
I SPENT A LOT OF BIRTHDAYS ON THE ROAD.
I DON'T MIND BECAUSE THE FANS GIVE ME
LOTS OF LOVE AND PRESENTS. —BRIAN

AJ AND ME LOOKING OUT THE BACK OF THE TOUR BUS IN GERMANY.
THIS WAS THE VERY FIRST TIME WE HAD OUR OWN POLICE ESCORT. —NICK

ONE OF OUR FIRST TRIPS TO MONTREAL. CANADA HAS BEEN GOOD TO US. —BRIAN

BRIAN BUILDING A SNOWMAN ON TOP OF NICK'S HEAD! —KEVIN

ON TOUR IN CANADA, WHICH CONTINUED
RIGHT AFTER OUR GERMAN TOUR. —HOWIE

DURING THE BAND INTRO. —BRIAN

WE CHANGED OUTFITS FOUR TIMES
DURING THESE SHOWS. WE ARE IN
OUR *FAME* OUTFITS. —AJ

MY FOOT GOT RUN OVER BY A MINIVAN. HERE I AM BEING CARRIED OFFSTAGE BY MY SECURITY SINCE I COULDN'T WALK. THE CUTE LITTLE RED-HAIRED WOMAN IN THE BACK IS MY MOM. —AJ

IS AJ TRYING TO TEACH NICK
HOW TO SHAVE? —KEVIN

ALL I CAN REMEMBER IS THAT
SOMEONE SHOVED A BIRTHDAY CAKE
IN MY FACE ON A TV SHOW IN
GERMANY AND I ENDED UP LOOKING
LIKE FATHER CHRISTMAS. —AJ

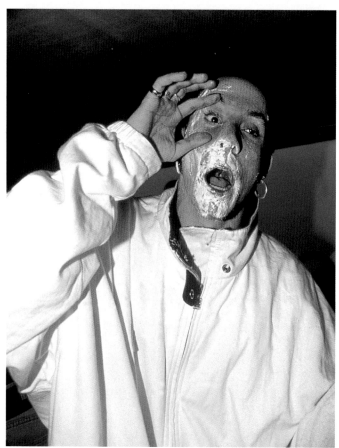

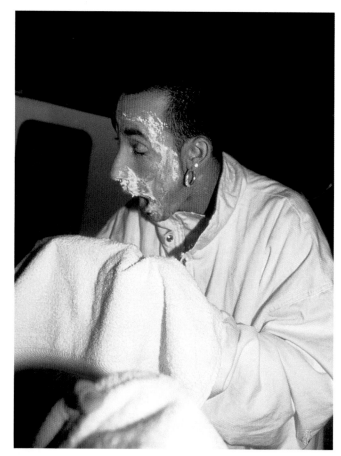

USING RANDY, MY BODYGUARD, AS A TABLE TO SIGN AUTOGRAPHS. —KEVIN

THE PRESSURE ON THE PLANE WAS TOO MUCH AND MY FOOT GOT SWOLLEN,
SO I TOOK MY SHOE OFF. I AM HOLDING THE SHOE IN MY HAND THINKING THAT I AM COOL.
NEVER DID GET AN ENDORSEMENT FROM THEM. —AJ

TWO PEAS IN A POD. I REMEMBER THAT LIKE IT WAS YESTERDAY. —BRIAN

ME AND AJ SLEEPING ON THE FLOOR DURING A PROMO TOUR OF GERMANY.
WE DIDN'T HAVE ANYWHERE TO CATCH UP ON SLEEP SO THE FLOOR WAS OK. —NICK

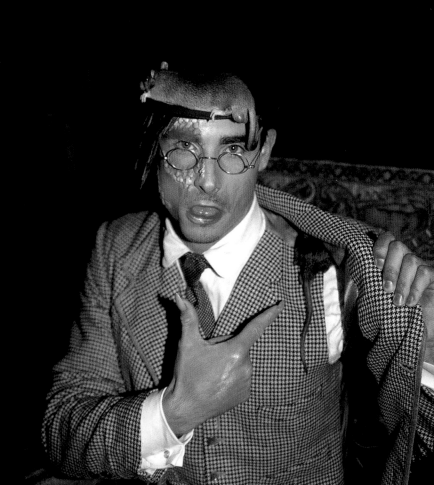

THIS IS THE ORIGINAL MAKE-
UP DESIGN FOR EACH OF US
IN THE "BACKSTREET'S BACK"
VIDEO. THIS IS JUST AN IDEA
OF WHAT EVERYBODY WOULD
LOOK LIKE. THE WHOLE MAKE-
UP WAS FIVE TIMES MORE
THAN IS SHOWN HERE AND IT
TOOK FIVE TIMES LONGER TO
DO IT. IT TOOK TWO TO THREE
HOURS FOR ME, AJ, AND
BRIAN AND UP TO SIX HOURS
FOR NICK AND KEVIN. —HOWIE

THIS IS RIGHT BEFORE WE DID THE ENDING SHOT OF THE VIDEO,
BEFORE WE SEE "HUGGY BEAR" AND SCREAM. —HOWIE

THIS WAS ONE OF THREE VIDEOS WE SHOT BACK-TO-BACK IN L.A. THEN GOT ON A PLANE,
FLEW TO LONDON, AND WENT RIGHT TO THE VENUE TO START OFF OUR EUROPEAN TOUR.
IT WAS CRAZY! —BSB

ON THE SET OF "ALL I HAVE TO GIVE." I'M MAKING
A FUNNY BEHIND HOWIE. HE WAS TRYING TO BE
SERIOUS. YOU KNOW ME. —BRIAN

"ALL I HAVE TO GIVE" VIDEO.
THIS IS A VERY CREATIVE SCENE THAT
DID NOT MAKE IT TO THE FINAL CUT.
THERE IS NO PHOTO OF BRIAN BECAUSE
WE RAN OUT OF TIME. —HOWIE

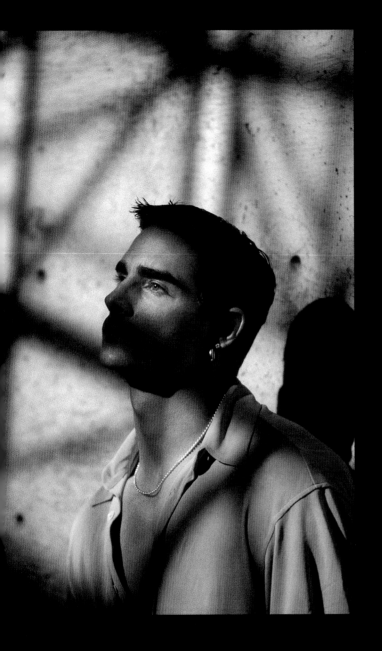

"AS LONG AS YOU LOVE ME"
VIDEO. NIGEL DICK DIRECTED.
LOT OF FUN. WHERE I MET THE
REST OF MY LIFE. —BRIAN

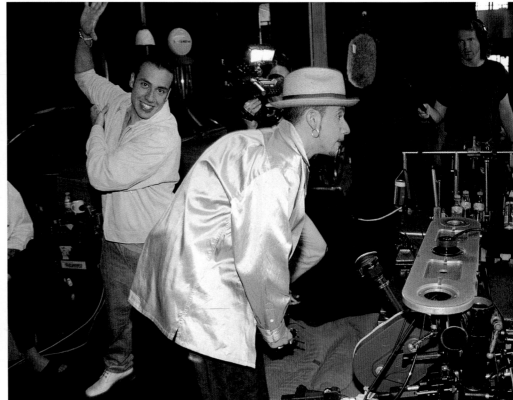

AS USUAL, I AM ACTING LIKE A GOOF. HOWIE IS TRYING TO SMACK ME.
VERY QUICK VIDEO SHOOT. WE CAME UP WITH THE IDEA FOR IT WITH
DIRECTOR NIGEL DICK. —AJ

WE WERE THINKING
ABOUT BECOMING
A PUNK BAND.
—KEVIN

THEY MADE ME
WEAR AN AFRO. I
DIDN'T WANT TO DO
IT, BUT AS A TEAM
MEMBER, I DID IT
FOR THE GROUP.
—HOWIE

THIS WAS BACK IN THE DAY.
THE STAGE FOR THE GERMAN OPEN-AIR TOUR.
IT WAS GREAT . . . WE HAD A BLAST. —NICK

THIS IS DURING REHEARSAL FOR
OUR GERMAN OPEN-AIR TOUR. THIS
WAS AN IDEA THAT OUR MANAGER
HAD. IT WAS GOING TO BE
ANNOUNCED THAT BSB COULDN'T
MAKE IT TO THE SHOW. THEN THIS
BOX WOULD BE ROLLED OUT WITH
A SIGN SAYING THE NAME OF A
COURIER COMPANY, AND WE WOULD
POP OUT OF IT AS IF WE WERE
SHIPPED IN TO DO THE SHOW. THE
IDEA DIDN'T WORK BECAUSE THE
RISER INSIDE THE BOX TOOK TOO
LONG TO LIFT US UP. —HOWIE

I'M HOLDING TORCHES, PRACTICING
FOR THE NEXT OLYMPIC GAMES.
—KEVIN

OUR GERMAN OPEN-AIR TOUR. THE STAGE HAD A LONG CATWALK THAT WENT TO A SMALLER STAGE IN THE CROWD.
DURING THE SONG "GET DOWN," I USED TO RUN THE LENGTH OF THE CATWALK AND JUMP ONTO THE SMALLER STAGE.
NOT THAT NIGHT! —AJ

WOW, THIS IS A COOL SHOT. JUST BEFORE THE GRAND FINALE BEFORE WE TAKE OUR BOWS. —BRIAN

WEMBLEY ARENA IN LONDON. IN OUR OUTFITS
FOR OUR INDIVIDUAL SONGS. —BRIAN

AND THAT'S WHO MAKES US WHO WE ARE,
THE BACKSTREET FANS. —BRIAN

BSB'S FIRST U.S. ALBUM RELEASE IN N.Y. DOING "BACKSTREET'S BACK" AT THE VIRGIN MEGASTORE IN THE MIDDLE
OF THE FANS AND THE VERY EXPENSIVE INVITATION TO OUR ALBUM LAUNCH AT THE VIRGIN MEGASTORE IN N.Y. —AJ

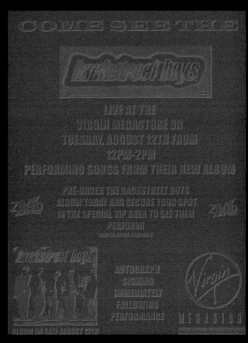

WE WERE FILMING A FOX
TV KIDS SHOW AT BUSCH
GARDENS. THE STUFFED
TEDDY BEARS WERE PART
OF A SKIT, AND I WAS
SUPPOSED TO RIDE WITH
THEM ON THE ROLLER
COASTER. —NICK

HERE WE WERE
ACTUALLY DOING THE
TEACUP RIDE. AS YOU
CAN SEE, I WAS GETTING
KIND OF SICK, AND
NICKY HAD A LOT OF
NACHOS. BETWEEN
THE RIDE AND THE
NACHOS, NO WONDER
I LOOK SICK. —HOWIE

IN MY MIAMI HEAT SHIRT, JUST AFTER WE REHEARSED. I REMEMBER GRABBING
ANDRE TO SNAP SOME PHOTOS IN FRONT OF THE FANS. —BRIAN

PERFORMANCE AT UNIVERSAL STUDIOS, FLORIDA. WE LOOK LIKE THE PIT CREW FOR NASCAR. —KEVIN

AT KISSIMMEE AIRPORT, WALKING TOWARD OUR VERY OWN BSB BLIMP. —NICK

THIS WAS EARLY ON DURING OUR U.S. TOUR . . . ONE OF OUR RARE DAYS OFF. BACK THEN WE COULD RELAX A LITTLE AND TRY TO DO NORMAL THINGS WITHOUT BEING RECOGNIZED. —BSB

THAT'S ME AND NINA, WHO WAS OUR TOUR MANAGER, AND DAVE THE TOUR ACCOUNTANT. HE HAD A LOAD OF MONEY WHICH WAS GOING TO BE OUR PER DIEMS AND I WAS FANTASIZING ABOUT TAKING IT ALL WHILE NINA BRIBED DAVE OFF WITH A BUCK TO GET IT FOR ME. —HOWIE

I TOOK THESE SHOTS ON THE ROOF
OF OUR HOTEL IN L.A. —BRIAN

A WINTERLAND
PHOTO SHOOT
OUTTAKE. —AJ

HOWIE, ME, AND U2'S
THE EDGE AT THE 1997 MTV
EUROPEAN AWARDS. —KEVIN

THIS IS US WITH
BLACKSTREET, ONE OF
OUR BIGGEST MUSICAL
INSPIRATIONS, AT THE
EUROPEAN MTV AWARDS.
—HOWIE

THIS WAS THE VERY FIRST TIME WE MET STEVEN TYLER.
WE'VE BECOME CLOSER AND CLOSER TO HIM OVER THE YEARS. —NICK

BRIAN PICKING ON ME AS USUAL. WE ALWAYS PICK ON EACH OTHER AND GET ON EACH OTHER'S CASES.
WE HAVE A BLAST, THOUGH. —NICK

TEASING NICK ON HIS SMASH HITS BEST HAIRCUT AWARD, AND STILL TEASING HIM
TODAY. GRAB HIS NECK, HE IS REALLY TICKLISH. —BRIAN

THE FIRST TIME WE
MET THE SPICE GIRLS,
THEIR DRESSING ROOM
WASN'T BIG ENOUGH
AND THEY TRIED TO
SHARE OURS BY
PUTTING A CURTAIN
DIVIDER UP. —AJ

MISS JANET.
—BRIAN

MEETING ONE OF MY IDOLS,
ELTON JOHN. A GREAT GUY. SINCE
THEN, WE HAVE RECORDED AND
PERFORMED WITH HIM. —KEVIN

AJ WITH HIS FAKE BLUE EYES IN . . . TRYING TO PICK BRIAN'S NOSE. —KEVIN

THE DUCHESS OF YORK,
SARAH FERGUSON, INTERVIEWED
US AT MTV STUDIOS IN NYC ON
MY EIGHTEENTH BIRTHDAY FOR
A MAGAZINE ARTICLE. —NICK

ON THE SET OF SABRINA,
THE TEENAGE WITCH. I'LL
NEVER FORGET THAT
SHOW, NOT THE MOST
COMFORTABLE SITUATION.
IT WAS THE FIRST TIME
THAT WE ALL HAD TO DO
SOME TYPE OF ACTING
TOGETHER. THEY GAVE ME
A BIRTHDAY CAKE SINCE
IT WAS MY BIRTHDAY
WEEK. —NICK

VIÑA DEL MAR, CHILE. COMING OFFSTAGE AFTER OUR SHOW. WE'D LOVE TO GO BACK. —BRIAN

THIS WAS TAKEN IN CHILE, OUTSIDE OUR HOTEL. WE WERE BANNED FROM LEAVING THE HOTEL BY THE POLICE BECAUSE THEY THOUGHT THERE WERE TOO MANY FANS. YOU'D HAVE THOUGHT MICHAEL JACKSON WAS STAYING THERE WITH THE AMOUNT OF SECURITY. ANYWAY, KEVIN, AJ, AND I DECIDED TO GO OUT. WE SHOULD HAVE LISTENED TO THE POLICE BECAUSE WHEN WE CAME BACK, THE FANS WENT BERSERK, AND I HAVE THE BATTLE WOUNDS TO PROVE IT. I WAS THE LAST ONE OUT OF THE VAN AND THE FANS CAUGHT ME AND WERE PULLING AT MY HAIR AND SCRATCHING ME ALL OVER. I STILL HAVE A SCAR ON THE BACK OF MY ARM TO REMIND ME OF THIS. —HOWIE

ARGENTINA. I THINK IT WAS ONE OF MY MOST PEACEFUL TIMES ON THE WHOLE TOUR. I SAT ON THE FRONT OF THE BOAT AND WAS JUST RELAXING, ENJOYING THE SUNSET. I AM USUALLY ONE WITH THE OCEAN AND NATURE. —NICK

BUENOS AIRES. UNBEKNOWNST TO ME, I CUT MY HAND ONSTAGE. EVERY TIME I WENT TO TOUCH A FAN'S HAND IN THE AUDIENCE, THEY WOULD GIVE ME FUNNY LOOKS AND NOT WANT TO TOUCH ME. THEN I LOOKED AT MY HAND AND SAW BLOOD EVERYWHERE. —KEVIN

SAN REMO, ITALY. WOW, LOOK AT ALL THE FANS.
THEY WERE INSANE, PACKED LIKE SARDINES. —AJ

THIS IS IN JAMAICA ON THE WAY TO THE AIRPORT. ONE OF THOSE TIMES WHEN I AM GAZING INTO SPACE . . . PROBABLY THINKING OF VIDEO GAMES. —NICK

I'M JOKING AROUND ON OUR PRIVATE JET ON THE WAY BACK FROM JAMAICA, WHERE WE FILMED AN MTV SHOW. —HOWIE

NEGRIL, JAMAICA, WITH CARMEN ELEKTRA.
I USED TO HAVE A CRUSH ON HER. —AJ

HERE'S A SWITCH. THIS IS AT A PHOTO SHOOT AND
ANDRE IS HANGING OUT IN THE BACKGROUND TAKING
A BREAK WHILE BRIAN TAKES PHOTOS FOR HIM. —BSB

———————————

ANOTHER PHOTO SHOOT. WITH THE STUDIO DOORSTOP, NIPPER. —AJ

HERE WE ARE AT WEMBLEY ARENA, LONDON. JUST VIBING AND CHILLING WITH OUR BAND FOR OUR FIRST VIVA UNPLUGGED SHOW TO BE RECORDED IN GERMANY. —NICK

THIS IS A RARE GLIMPSE OF MY STOMACH. I DON'T USUALLY SHOW IT BECAUSE I AM TUMMY SHY. —NICK

AJ AT VIVA WITH HIS NEW LOOK. —KEVIN

MY IDEA WAS THAT THE UNPLUGGED SHOW SHOULD BE MORE INTIMATE, SO I GRABBED THE CARPET AND LAID IT ON THE STAGE TO CREATE THAT INTIMATE EFFECT. EVERYBODY THOUGHT I WAS CRAZY AND DIDN'T KNOW WHAT I WAS TALKING ABOUT, BUT IT TURNED OUT REALLY GOOD. —NICK

WHO IS THE GUY IN THE MIDDLE? LOOKS LIKE A GOOD STAGEHAND. LET'S GET HIM FOR THE NEXT TOUR. —BRIAN

THE GUYS ARE ALWAYS PLAYING PRACTICAL JOKES ON ME WHILE I CATCH SOME SLEEP,
DECORATING ME WITH COOKIES AND OTHER THINGS. THEY THINK IT'S FUNNY. I DON'T REALLY THINK SO.
WARNING: YOU MIGHT SEE MORE SHOTS OF ME SLEEPING. —HOWIE

WE DID THE "I'LL NEVER BREAK YOUR HEART" VIDEO IN ENGLISH AND SPANISH. —HOWIE

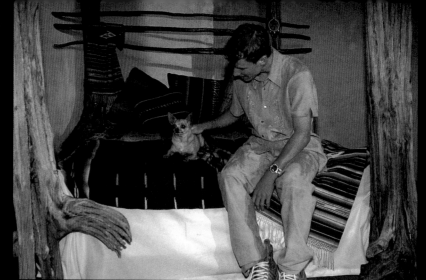

ON THE VIDEO SET
WITH A CHIHUAHUA
JUST BEFORE I GOT
TIKE. —BRIAN

THIS IS ON THE SET OF THE "I'LL NEVER BREAK YOUR HEART" VIDEO. I'M SITTING NEAR THE STORYBOARD.
DISCUSSING THE SHOTS WE WERE GOING TO DO ON THE SHOOT. I WAS A BIT WORRIED ABOUT THE FACT THAT
GOING TO BE THE FIRST TIME THAT WE WERE DOING INTIMATE SCENES WITH GIRLS IN A VIDEO. —NI

THIS WAS IN
MEXICO DURING A
PROMOTIONAL TRIP
I TOOK ON BEHALF
OF BSB. I WENT TO
THE PYRAMIDS JUST
OUTSIDE MEXICO CITY.
—HOWIE

MY FAVORITE FOOTBALL TEAM JERSEY. I AM LAUGHING AT BRIAN'S GUITAR PLAYING. EVENTUALLY IT GOT BETTER. —NICK

IS THAT ME? —NICK

CANADA, TRYING TO FIND OUT HOW TALL THE GRIM REAPER WAS IN OUR SHOW. I WASN'T EVEN CLOSE. —BRIAN

WITH VENUS AND SERENA WILLIAMS. TENNIS IS ONE OF MY PASSIONS.
IT'S A CHALLENGING SPORT. —BRIAN

———————

THIS IS MY WAY OF GETTING EVEN WITH NICK WHEN HE AGGRAVATES ME. —HOWIE

WOULD YOU BUY A CAR FROM THIS MAN?
LAS VEGAS. IN FRONT OF MY DREAM CAR,
A PROWLER, USED AS A PROP ON A
PHOTO SHOOT FOR A MAGAZINE. KEVIN IS
PRETENDING TO GIVE ME THE KEYS. —AJ

LAS VEGAS, BEFORE OUR FIRST APPEARANCE
AT THE MGM GRAND. —HOWIE

LIVING IT UP IN THE BATH, IN MY SUITE AT THE MGM GRAND IN VEGAS . . .

. . . UNTIL OUR TOUR MANAGER AND MY MOM DUNKED ME. —AJ

"THE FONZ, HEYYYYYYYY." THAT'S WHAT WE'RE SAYING WITH HENRY WINKLER. —BRIAN

WITH JENNIFER LOVE HEWITT AT THE UNIVERSAL AMPHITHEATER IN L.A. BEFORE OUR SHOW. SHE JUST SIGNED RECENTLY WITH OUR RECORD LABEL. —AJ

BRIAN AND I
APPROVING
PICTURES IN
CANADA.
—HOWIE

NICK APPROVING A PHOTO,
YEAH RIGHT. —BRIAN

MY MOM. BEING SYMPATHETIC AT MY LATEST MISHAP. AT OUR DOUBLE SHOW IN TORONTO DURING "GET DOWN," I RIPPED MY QUAD MUSCLE AND COULDN'T PERFORM FOR A FEW SHOWS. —AJ

MR. CANE MEISTER. —BRIAN

THE GUYS PLAYED A JOKE AND HAD A CARDBOARD CUTOUT OF ME ONSTAGE. —AJ

IN ARGENTINA ON OUR WAY TO THE SHOW. THE FANS WENT BERSERK AND BROKE THE BUS WINDOW RIGHT IN FRONT OF ME. —HOWIE

OUR AWESOME FANS IN SOUTH AMERICA, PEOPLE ON MOTORCYCLES AND HANGING OUT OF THEIR CARS. IT WAS TOTALLY CRAZY. WE WERE BLOWN AWAY BY THEIR RECEPTION. —KEVIN

THIS WAS ONE OF THE MOST SCARY TIMES AS FANS WERE FOLLOWING US IN A HIGH-SPEED CHASE, HANGING OUT OF THEIR CAR ROOFS AND WINDOWS. —NICK

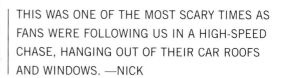

ALL THE FANS AND PRESS FOLLOWING US ON THE HIGHWAY. —HOWIE

WITH VANESSA MAE, THE VIOLINIST, WHO DID A
NUMBER WITH US IN BUENOS AIRES. —KEVIN

WITH DIEGO MARADONNA, HUGE SOCCER
PLAYER FROM ARGENTINA. —HOWIE

BUENOS AIRES. HOW ABOUT A QUIET GOLF GAME? AS YOU CAN SEE, WE WERE FOLLOWED.
NORMALLY GOLF IS A QUIET SPORT. —BRIAN

IN THE STUDIO WITH PRODUCER STEVE LIPSON, RECORDING "BACK TO YOUR HEART,"
IN LONDON ON MY BIRTHDAY IN 1998. —KEVIN

STUDYING SOME WORDS
BEFORE RECORDING WITH
KEV FOR THE *MILLENNIUM*
ALBUM. —AJ

RECORDING AT PARC STUDIOS IN ORLANDO. —NICK

RECORDING IN STOCKHOLM. I WAS SINGING "DON'T WANT TO LOSE YOU NOW." —HOWIE

THIS IS IN DESERT SPRINGS BY AN ABANDONED GAS STATION IN THE MIDDLE OF NOWHERE. —HOWIE

TAKING OUT MY FRUSTRATION ON A LONG, HARD PHOTO SHOOT. —NICK

MEAT LOAF. MY MAN. I LOVE HIM.
ONE OF MY FAVORITE ARTISTS. —NICK

WITH GARTH BROOKS AT THE *BILLBOARD*
AWARDS IN VEGAS. HE ASKED ME IF WE
WERE PERFORMING, TOLD HIM NO, NOT THIS
YEAR, HOPEFULLY NEXT YEAR. HE REPLIED,
"IF THEY'RE LUCKY." THAT WAS COOL. WE
GOT THE IDEA OF FLYING IN OUR SHOW
FROM WATCHING HIM. —KEVIN

WE FILMED DICK CLARK'S
NEW YEAR'S EVE SHOW IN
LAS VEGAS. IT WAS LOTS OF
FUN AND WAS THE FIRST
TIME WE MET DICK. SOME
OF US GREW UP WATCHING
AMERICAN BANDSTAND AND
ARE FANS OF HIS. —HOWIE

ORLANDO ARENA ON NEW YEAR'S EVE. WE PERFORMED PRINCE'S "1999." —NICK

IN OUR HOMETOWN . . . OUR FIRST-EVER PERFORMANCE AT THE ORLANDO ARENA
ON NEW YEAR'S EVE. IT WAS LOTS OF FUN AND A DREAM COME TRUE, ESPECIALLY FOR ME TO PERFORM
AT THE PLACE WHERE I SAW MY VERY FIRST CONCERT. —HOWIE

BUSTING MY BUTT.
WE WERE SHOOTING
FOR THE AMERICAN
MUSIC AWARDS. —KEVIN

MY TWENTY-FIRST BIRTHDAY PARTY. HOLLYWOOD. —AJ

THE *MILLENNIUM* ALBUM COVER PHOTO SHOOT WAS DONE IN AND AROUND A HAUNTED MANSION IN THE L.A. HILLS. PARTS OF *HALLOWEEN H2O* WERE SHOT THERE. —HOWIE

THIS IS ONE OF MY FAVORITE PLACES. I HAD A BLAST IN THAT MANSION. I ACTUALLY RAN AROUND THE HOUSE WITH A POLAROID CAMERA AT NIGHT TAKING PICTURES EVERYWHERE, TRYING TO FIND THE GHOST, BUT I COULDN'T. —NICK

THIS IS SOMETHING THAT I PARTICULARLY WANTED FOR THE ARTWORK FOR THE ALBUM. I WANTED MY PICTURES TO DO WITH WATER. MY ELEMENT. —NICK

WOW, THIS WAS A LOT OF FUN. RECORDING OF "PERFECT FAN." GOT THE CHANCE TO SHARE MY DREAMS WITH A LOT OF FRIENDS BACK HOME. ALL MY FRIENDS FROM TATES CREEK HIGH SCHOOL CHOIR, LEXINGTON, KENTUCKY, HELPED ME RECORD THIS SONG. —BRIAN

OUT IN THE TRUCK LISTENING BACK TO THE RECORDING. —BRIAN

HERE I AM GETTING
TO REALIZE ONE
OF MY BIGGEST
DREAMS: FLYING A
FIGHTER JET. IT'S
ONE OF THE MOST
INCREDIBLE EXPERI-
ENCES IN MY LIFE.
WHAT A RUSH. IT'S
LIKE DRIVING A
SPORTS CAR IN THE
AIR. I AM ALSO
SHOWN IN CASE I
AM GOING TO BE
SICK, THERE'S
THE BARF BAG.
—KEVIN

AJ SOAKED NICK BY HITTING THE FAUCET AT HIS ELBOW. —BRIAN

IT WAS RAINING ON THAT DAY IN PARIS AND I WAS AROUND THE CORNER FROM THE HOTEL. THERE WERE HUNDREDS OF FANS OUTSIDE THE HOTEL BUT THEY NEVER SAW ME TAKING THESE PICTURES A FEW HUNDRED YARDS AWAY FROM THEM.
—HOWIE

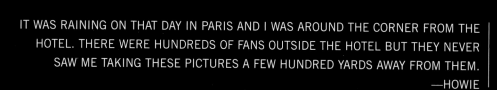

MY ATTEMPT AT JOINING SPINAL TAP. —AJ

NICK EXPERIMENTING WITH HIS NEW HAIRDO. —KEVIN

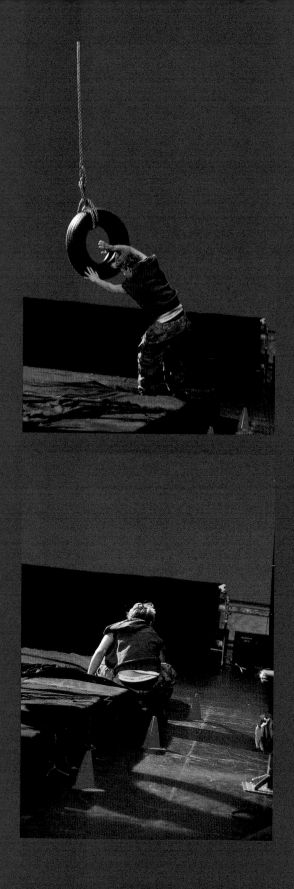

THIS WAS THE PROMO SHOOT FOR THE *MILLENNIUM* ALBUM. IT TURNED OUT VERY FUNNY. —NICK

I'M PAINTED ALL UP AS A GLADIATOR. THE HELMET WEIGHED FORTY POUNDS. THEY WANTED ME TO HOLD IT RATHER THAN WEAR IT. —BRIAN

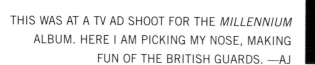

THIS WAS AT A TV AD SHOOT FOR THE *MILLENNIUM* ALBUM. HERE I AM PICKING MY NOSE, MAKING FUN OF THE BRITISH GUARDS. —AJ

AS YOU CAN SEE, THE MUSIC BUSINESS
CAN TAKE ITS TOLL ON YOU. —KEVIN

I AM TAKING ON THE FANS RUNNING AT US DURING A COMMERCIAL SHOOT FOR THE U.S. TOUR SPONSORS. REALLY I WAS OUT OF MY MIND. —NICK

OF COURSE, WITH OUR LUCK IT RAINED THE WHOLE TIME WE FILMED OUTSIDE. —HOWIE

OUR INCREDIBLE FANS SHUT DOWN TIMES SQUARE DURING OUR MTV APPEARANCE FOR THE LAUNCH OF *MILLENNIUM*. THE POLICE ALMOST THREW US OUT OF THE STUDIOS. WE WEREN'T ALLOWED NEAR THE WINDOWS TO WAVE AT THEM. WHAT AN INCREDIBLE DAY IT WAS. —KEVIN

WITH ALICE COOPER LATER AT OUR ALBUM LAUNCH PARTY. —KEVIN

MY MOM GOT TO MEET HIM. —AJ

———————

SATURDAY NIGHT LIVE WITH THE CAST OF *BUFFY THE VAMPIRE SLAYER*.
WE PERFORMED ON THE SHOW AND I DID A SEPARATE SKIT ON MY OWN. —HOWIE

I JUST GOT THE NEWS DURING REHEARSALS IN NASHVILLE FOR OUR EUROPEAN TOUR THAT OUR SINGLE "LARGER THAN LIFE" WENT TO #1 IN THE U.K. IT WAS OUR FIRST #1 IN THE U.K. AFTER SEVERAL YEARS OF TRYING.
—HOWIE

MY FIRST EXPERIENCE FLYING IN A HARNESS OVER AN ARENA. I WAS SCARED. IT'S A WEIRD FEELING HAVING MY BODY ELEVATED AND SWINGING OUT OVER THE AUDIENCE. OF COURSE, AJ AND EVERYBODY ELSE ARE LAUGHING AT ME. —HOWIE

NASHVILLE, REHEARSING FOR THE EUROPEAN LEG OF THE *MILLENNIUM* TOUR. WE HAD TO SHUT DOWN THE REHEARSALS FOR A HURRICANE WATCH AND THEN CANCEL THE OPENING OF OUR U.S. TOUR IN FORT LAUDERDALE FOUR MONTHS LATER FOR THE SAME REASON. —AJ

BRIAN AND I AT AJAX STADIUM IN HOLLAND. WE WERE SUPPOSED TO PLAY BASKETBALL
THERE ON AN INDOOR COURT, BUT IT TURNED OUT THEY DIDN'T HAVE ONE.
THIS IS ONE OF THE BIGGEST STADIUMS IN THE WORLD. —NICK

———————————

AJAX STADIUM, AMSTERDAM, WHERE NICK AND I HAD OUR PICTURE TAKEN THE YEAR BEFORE.
THEY TOOK THE GRASS UP AND THERE YOU HAVE IT. —BRIAN

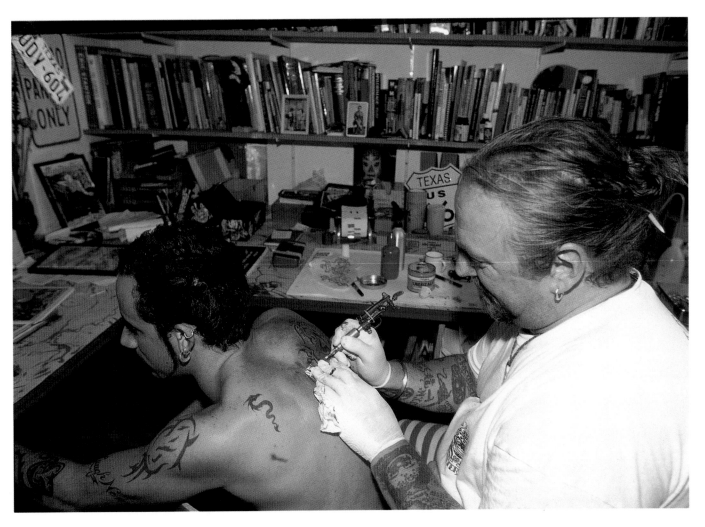

WITH THE GREATEST TATTOO ARTIST
OF HIS TIME, MR. HANKY PANKY IN
AMSTERDAM. HE DOES HIS WORK
AT HOME AND WHILE I WAITED FOR
HIM TO START, I COOKED MYSELF
BREAKFAST. HE TATTOOED A
DRAGON ON MY RIGHT SHOULDER.
I HOPE TO GET MORE TATTOOS
FROM HIM WHEN I GO BACK. —AJ

BABY SPICE VISITED US IN LONDON BEFORE
THE SHOW AT EARLS COURT. —AJ

IN ROME WITH GEORGE LUCAS. WE USE THE *STAR
WARS* THEME TO OPEN THE SHOW AND WE NEVER
ASKED HIM IF WE COULD. I HEARD LATER THAT HE
WAS PLEASED THAT WE USED IT. I ASKED HIM IF HE
WOULD CONSIDER DIRECTING OUR NEXT VIDEO,
"LARGER THAN LIFE," BUT UNFORTUNATELY, HE WAS
TIED UP WITH HIS NEXT *STAR WARS* PROJECT. —HOWIE

IN A SOCCER FIELD IN ROME FOR AN OUTDOOR SHOW.
—KEVIN

PISA, ITALY. AJ AND I WENT OUT
TO DO A LITTLE SIGHTSEEING.
—HOWIE

KEVIN AND I DECIDED TO SWIM A HALF MILE OUT TO OUR DANCERS WHO GOT STUCK ON LAKE GARDA. WE ENDED UP HITCHING A RIDE BACK. —NICK

WE WERE AT A PRIVATE PARTY ON OUR DAY OFF IN ITALY NEAR LAKE COMO. NICKY INSISTED ON THROWING ME IN THE POOL, BUT AS YOU CAN SEE, NICKY GOT A BIGGER SURPRISE THAN ME. —HOWIE

PRACTICING
KEYBOARDS. I TRY
TO DO A SOUND
CHECK AS OFTEN
AS I CAN. —KEVIN

HERE I AM FLYING THE U.S. FLAG DURING OUR SHOW. —KEVIN

THE STAGE FOR OUR NEW SHOW.—BSB

THIS IS A MINIATURE OF
OUR STAGE FOR THE
NEW SHOW. WE DECIDED
TO DO IT IN THE ROUND
BUT THE STAGE ITSELF
IS A PENTAGON. —KEVIN

ZARAGOZA, SPAIN. JUST
AFTER WE LAND ONSTAGE, WE
WALK AROUND. THEN
"LARGER THAN LIFE" KICKS
IN AND SO DOES THE PYRO.
—HOWIE

THIS IS THE END OF
OUR SHOW. WE NEVER
GET TO SEE THIS AS WE
ARE RUNNING FOR THE
BUS BY THE TIME THE
PYRO STARTS. —AJ

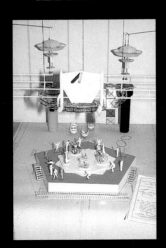

IN BARCELONA WITH JAMES HETFIELD OF METALLICA. I WAS TRYING
MY HARDEST NOT TO LOOK EXCITED AND NOT ACT LIKE A FAN, BUT
INSIDE I WANTED TO EXPLODE BECAUSE HE WAS THERE. —NICK

MADRID, WITH AN INCREDIBLE ACTOR, BRUCE WILLIS.
HE CAME TO CHECK OUT THE SHOW. —AJ

I WAS ATTEMPTING TO PLAY SOCCER IN SCANDINAVIA WITH
THE BAND, BUT WE GOT OUR BUTTS KICKED. —NICK

IN SCANDINAVIA DOING SOME PRESS IN THE ARENA ABOVE THE STAGE. —HOWIE

THIS WAS THE LAST NIGHT
OF THE TOUR. —HOWIE

END-OF-TOUR "LAST SHOW JOKES." HERE'S KEVIN GIVING US THE EYEBROWS. —BSB

OUR SAX PLAYER AND I GOT INTO A BIG WATER FIGHT. —NICK

THE STRANGE BLOND-HAIRED FREAK NEXT TO ME IS ONE OF THE MOST INCREDIBLE MUSICAL GENIUSES, MR. MAX MARTIN, WHO PRODUCED MANY HIT SONGS, INCLUDING "QUIT PLAYING GAMES" AND

ONE OF MY MOST FAVORITE VIDEO SHOOTS. THEY LITERALLY HAD TO CONSTRUCT MY ROBOT OUTFIT ON ME. I DESIGNED IT MYSELF WITH THE COSTUME DESIGNER. —NICK

BEING WRAPPED IN PLASTIC WRAP AT THE "LARGER THAN LIFE" SHOOT. GETTING READY TO BLAST OFF IN MY TIME CAPSULE. —KEVIN

THREE A.M. AFTER MY SCENE IN THE "LARGER THAN LIFE" VIDEO, KINDA LOOKING LIKE A MARSHMALLOW MAN. —HOWIE

MOSTLY SHOT IN FRONT OF A GREEN SCREEN WITH COMPUTER ANIMATIONS ADDED LATER. IN MY SCENE, I AM WEARING ABOUT FIFTY POUNDS OF PLASTIC AND HUNG IN THE AIR FOR HOURS WITH NO REST ROOM TIME OUT. NOT VERY COMFORTABLE. I WAS NUMB FOR DAYS. —AJ

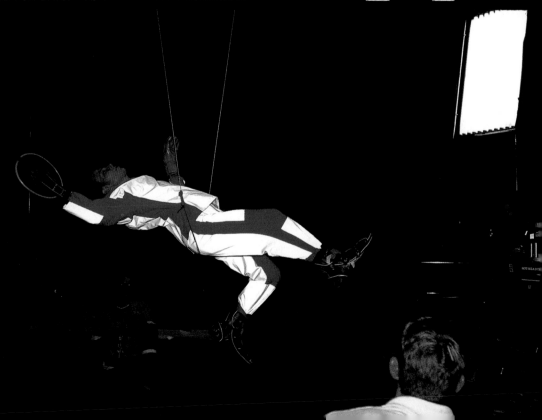

PLAYING MY FUTURISTIC RAG BALL STUFF ON THE "LARGER THAN LIFE" SET IN ORLANDO. —BRIAN

REHEARSING FOR THE 1999 MTV AWARDS IN N.Y. —AJ

DURING THE MTV AWARDS WEEK IN NEW YORK, WE WERE HONORED
BY HAVING A BSB STREET NAMED AFTER US. —HOWIE

WITH CLOSE PERSONAL FRIEND BIG BOB.
I USUALLY HOP ON HIS BACK. THIS WAY,
I CAN GET NEAR THE FANS WITHOUT
GETTING MAIMED. —AJ

LEXINGTON, RUPP ARENA, ME AND MY MOM
DURING "PERFECT FAN." I WROTE THE
SONG FOR HER. —BRIAN

WITH MY MOTHER ONSTAGE IN
LEXINGTON, KENTUCKY. I AM TRYING NOT
TO CRY TOO MUCH. —KEVIN

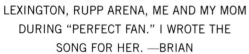

WITH PRINCE ANDREW AT THE RYDER CUP PARTY IN BOSTON,
SIGNING AUTOGRAPHS FOR HIS KIDS. —HOWIE

WITH TIGER WOODS AND PRINCE ANDREW HANGING
AND GETTING TO KNOW EACH OTHER. —HOWIE

WITH GENE SIMMONS AT THE FORUM SHOW IN L.A. PRACTICING HIS
FAMOUS TONGUE-TO-THE-GROUND TRADEMARK. —KEVIN

AT OUR HOTEL IN LAGUNA BEACH DURING THE U.S. TOUR. —BRIAN

YOU GOTTA LOVE MY PANTS. KEV AND I
AT PEBBLE BEACH, CALIFORNIA. —AJ

PEBBLE BEACH WITH MY DAD. IT WAS HIS
FIFTIETH BIRTHDAY, SO I FLEW HIM OUT TO PLAY
WITH ME. I AM A LEFTY AND HE IS A RIGHTY
IF YOU LOOK CLOSELY. —BRIAN

KEVIN, NICE FORM, LOOKS A GOOD SHOT. LEFT ARM STIFF, NOT BAD. RIGHT OUT OF THE TEE BOX. —BRIAN

HALLOWEEN IN DENVER.
TRYING ON COSTUMES AFTER
I HURT MY SHOULDER
SNOWBOARDING. —KEVIN

GRACELAND.
I AM A BIG ELVIS FAN. —AJ

THE ONLY TIME THAT I DON'T
LIKE BEING BOTHERED IS WHEN
I EAT. HERE WE ARE IN NEW
ORLEANS WITH HOWIE, MY MOM
AND UNCLE, AND THE WHOLE
TIME WE WERE WATCHED AND
IT MADE ME FEEL VERY
UNCOMFORTABLE. —AJ

WITH NICK WORKING ON AN
ELTON JOHN SONG FOR THE
MOVIE *EL DORADO* DURING
THE U.S. TOUR. —AJ

IN NASHVILLE WITH WYNONNA JUDD. WE HAD MET HER BEFORE IN VEGAS.
SHE IS REAL COOL. —HOWIE

HULKSTER. HIS ARM IS AS BIG AS MY HEAD. —BRIAN AND NICK

DURING THE LAST SONG, I ALWAYS TRY TO GO DOWN TO THE AUDIENCE AND WALK AROUND THE PIT
IN FRONT OF THE STAGE AND SHAKE AS MANY HANDS AS POSSIBLE. —HOWIE

TRYING TO BE A "HE MAN" AND NOT
WAIT FOR SECURITY WHEN WE RUN
FROM THE STAGE TO THE DRESSING
ROOM. I GOT MAULED. WASN'T A
GOOD IDEA. —HOWIE

UNDER THE *MILLENNIUM* STAGE, CHANGING INTO OUR WHITE OUTFITS FOR THE "BACKSTREET'S BACK/WE'VE GOT IT GOING ON" MEDLEY. IT'S DIFFICULT BECAUSE WE DO NOT HAVE MUCH SPACE TO DO IT IN AND THINGS KEEP MOVING ONSTAGE, BEING LOWERED, ETC. WE ALWAYS BUMP OUR HEAD ON SOMETHING. —AJ

RISING WITH THE PIANO, HOPING IT WORKS. —KEVIN

UNDERNEATH THE STAGE CHANGING COSTUMES FOR "DON'T WANT YOU BACK." —HOWIE

TRYING TO BEAT STEVEN TYLER WITH THE
CRAZIEST-LOOKING HAIRDO AT THE *BILLBOARD*
AWARDS. DIDN'T QUITE SUCCEED. —NICK

WITH JAMES HETFIELD AT THE *BILLBOARD* AWARDS.
NICK'S A HUGE METALLICA FAN. —HOWIE

THERE'S MY MAN AGAIN. METALLICA PRESENTED
US WITH THE "BAND OF THE YEAR" AWARD. —NICK

GETTING MY THIRD TATTOO DONE. ONE OF MY FAVORITE TATTOOS
BESIDES THE SHARK. IT DIDN'T HURT THAT BAD. —NICK

SHOW ME THE MEANING" VIDEO. TYPICAL
THREE-DAY VIDEO SHOOT WHERE I DIDN'T GET
ANY SLEEP. BELIEVE IT OR NOT, BUT I FELL
ASLEEP STANDING UP AROUND 5 A.M., LEANING
ON A CONE, AND AS USUAL WHEN I FALL
ASLEEP, THERE IS A PICTURE OF IT. —HOWIE

SOUND CHECK AT THE HARD ROCK LIVE GETTING READY FOR MY FIRST JOHNNY SUEDE PERFORMANCE ON MY TWENTY-SECOND BIRTHDAY. B-ROK DID ME A FAVOR BY GETTING ONSTAGE FOR TWO SONGS. —AJ

BRIAN GIVING ME A FEW WORDS OF ADVICE BEFORE THE START OF THE SHOW. WE HAD A QUICK LITTLE PRAYER TOGETHER, THE CURTAINS WENT UP, AND JOHNNY SUEDE WAS BORN. —AJ

JOHNNY NO NAME IS MY CURRENT NAME. *JOHNNY SUEDE* WAS A MOVIE WITH BRAD PITT. THE DIRECTOR OF THE FILM WOULD NOT ALLOW ME TO USE THAT NAME UNLESS I PAID HIM A LOT OF MONEY. JOHNNY SUEDE–NO NAME SAYS BE COOL, BE REAL, AND BEHAVE, BABY. —AJ

FUN AND GAMES DURING REHEARSALS. —BSB

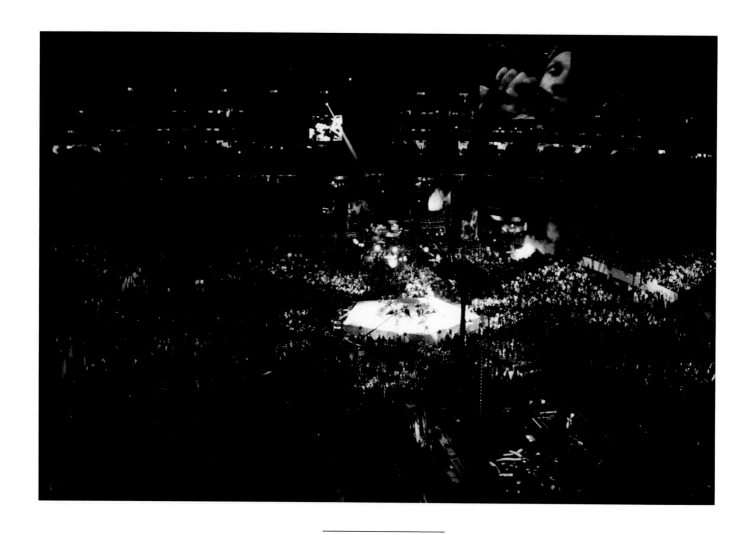

GEORGIA DOME. ONE OF THE BIGGEST VENUES WE EVER PLAYED
IN THE U.S. I WAS TELLING KEVIN HOW EXCITING IT WAS TO
FINALLY BE AT THE POINT WHERE WE COULD PLAY SHOWS OF
THIS MAGNITUDE IN THE U.S. —NICK

HERE WE ARE WITH SIR ELTON JOHN AT THIS YEAR'S GRAMMYS.
WE WERE REALLY EXCITED TO BE NOMINATED FOR
FIVE AWARDS. —BSB

WITH SIR ELTON PERFORMING ONE OF HIS HUGE HITS
AT THE 2000 GRAMMYS, "PHILADELPHIA FREEDOM." HE ACTUALLY
ASKED US TO PERFORM AND IT WAS BEYOND AN HONOR
TO WORK WITH HIM. —AJ

backstreet boys